SKIES IN BLOSSOM

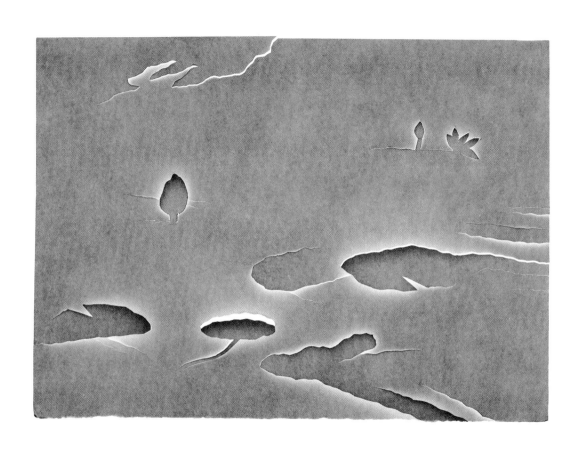

SKIES IN BLOSSOM

The Nature Poetry of Emily Dickinson

Edited by Jonathan Cott
Illustrated by Mary Frank

DOUBLEDAY

New York   London   Toronto
Sydney   Auckland

PUBLISHED BY DOUBLEDAY

a division of Bantam Doubleday Dell Publishing Group, Inc.
1540 Broadway, New York, New York 10036

DOUBLEDAY *and the portrayal of an anchor with a*
dolphin are trademarks of Doubleday, a division of Bantam Doubleday
Dell Publishing Group, Inc.

Book design by Marysarah Quinn

Library of Congress Cataloging-in-Publication Data
Dickinson, Emily, 1830–1886.
Skies in blossom : the nature poetry of Emily Dickinson / Emily Dickinson ; edited by
Jonathan Cott ; illustrated by Mary Frank. — 1st ed.
p.   cm.
1. Nature—Poetry.   I. Cott, Jonathan.   II. Frank, Mary, 1933–
III. Title.
PS1541.A6   1995a
811'.4—dc20   *94-48083*
                                                                        CIP

ISBN 0-385-47595-0
Text of introduction copyright © 1995 by Jonathan Cott
Artwork copyright © 1995 by Mary Frank
All Rights Reserved
Printed in the United States of America
October 1995

10   9   8   7   6   5   4   3   2   1

FIRST EDITION

IN MEMORY OF OUR EDITOR
JACQUELINE KENNEDY ONASSIS

Unable are the loved — to die —
For love is immortality —
Nay — it is Deity —

(EMILY DICKINSON)

SKIES IN BLOSSOM

I rather think I see myself walk up
A flight of wooden steps and ring a bell
And send a card in to Miss Dickinson.
Yet that's a very silly way to do.
I should have taken the dream twist-ends about
And climbed over the fence and found her deep
Engrossed in the doing of a humming-bird
Among nasturtiums . . .

—AMY LOWELL

t is said that Shākyamuni Buddha once gave a lecture on Vulture Peak Mountain in the sixth century B.C. to more than a thousand of his disciples in which he simply held up a flower without saying a word. Only his student Kāshyapa grasped the "meaning" of unmediated being, smiled, and achieved illumination. Some twenty-four hundred years later, in Amherst, Massachusetts, the American poet Emily Dickinson wrote:

Some keep the Sabbath going to Church —
I keep it, staying at Home —
With a Bobolink for a Chorister —
And an Orchard, for a Dome —

In the orchard outside her kitchen door, she "interpreted" the flowers, "which," she noted, "without lips, have language"—a language that "spoke" to her as it did to Buddha's student.

Like all those who can see heaven in a wildflower, Emily Dickinson lived a life of illumination. She paid scant heed to her Amherst neighbors who derisively referred to her as the "Queen Recluse" and declared her to be "cracked"; for as Edith Sitwell commented about a similarly disparaged William Blake, "The crack was where the light came through." Spending her days in silence, solitude, and contemplation, Dickinson lived the life of the spiritual seer who knows that experience is its own transcendence and that all beings are in nirvana from the start. All that is required to become aware of this, she once remarked, is *not* "Revelation" but only "our unfurnished eyes."

There are, of course, many Emily Dickinsons; and not every one of her interpreters has considered her a disciple of the Buddha. In *The Belle of Amherst* the playwright William Luce portrays Dickinson as a whimsical, eccentric spinster, sewing and cooking and baking her father's bread, mending slippers, and tending to her plants and flowers. In *After Great Pain* the psychiatrist Dr. John Cody asserts that she suffered from clinical depression, depersonalization, estrangement, thought disorder, and at least one major psychotic breakdown. In *Emily Dickinson: Woman Poet* Paula Bennett suggests that the writer's love for her sister-in-law, Susan Gilbert, was the central emotional experience of her life; and Bennett emphasizes the "richness and beauty of the homoerotic strain in Dickinson's writing." In *The Marriage of Emily Dickinson* William H. Shurr argues that in her mid-twenties, Dickinson fell in love with her counselor/therapist, the Reverend Charles Wadsworth, pledged herself to him in spiritual marriage, their hoped-for "union in heaven" a reward for their separation during life. And in *The Madwoman in the Attic* Sandra M. Gilbert explains Emily Dickinson's habitual recourse to white dress—her "Uniforms of Snow"—as her means of embodying the characters of virgin, nun, bride, madwoman, dead woman, and ghost. White is the product of the convergence of all the colors of the spectrum, a purity containing all. So it is ironic but not surprising that in the twentieth century this poet of various selves has become Everybody's Emily.

In her own time Emily Dickinson (1830–86) was for most of her life an agoraphobic and recluse. She once described herself as "small, like the Wren, and my Hair, is bold like the Chestnut Bur – and my eyes, like the sherry in the Glass, that the Guest leaves"; and she lived in a corner bedroom on the second floor of her family's brick mansion overlooking Main Street in Amherst, Massachusetts. Here in her room containing a bed, a Sheraton bureau, a Franklin stove, and a cherry table with one drawer, she wrote 1,775 poems (only 7 of which were published during her lifetime) on various scraps of paper and on the backs of recipes, shopping lists, clippings, and invitations, as well as more than a thousand letters to relatives, friends, and correspondents that in their beauty, profundity, spiritual insight, and penetration into the creative process rival those of John Keats and Vincent van Gogh.

Legend has it that during the last fifteen years of her life Emily Dickinson left her house only once, and that was at night, to creep out and view a new church by moonlight. When delivery boys from town came to the house, she would disappear and let someone else answer the door. When a pianist or singer entertained in the downstairs drawing room, she would stand in the darkened stairway, unobserved, listen to the music, and, as a token of appreciation, send down to the artist a silver salver bearing a glass of wine or sherry, a flower, and sometimes an impromptu poem. She occasionally let children individually into the house for a piece of candy, but more often chose to play with them by lowering cookies and gingerbread in a basket from her bedroom window. In later years her little niece Mattie recalled standing in front of her aunt's room as Dickinson held up an imaginary key and with a quick motion of her wrist declared, "It's just a turn — and freedom, Mattie!"

Choosing not to leave her father's home, Emily Dickinson

transformed the room-of-her-own—with what she called its sense of "Finite Infinity"—into an anchorite's cell, containing, as she described it, "my little Lamp, and Book—/And one Geranium." But if Emily chose the life of a postulant, it was not in any traditional Christian sense. As a teenager studying at Mount Holyoke Female Seminary, she found herself incapable of joining her enthusiast classmates in making the commitment to Christ as Savior. Of the three groups in her school, "Christians," "Hopers" (those considered close to making a commitment), and "No-hopers," Emily was irredeemably counted among the third. She grew up in a surcharged Puritan environment that valued austerity, simplicity, introspection, hard work, denial of the flesh. Although all of these played a significant part in her life, she steadfastly rejected the doctrines of predestination and original sin and doubted the idea of redemption. She paid no regard to the frequent religious revivals in Amherst and, to her mother's extreme displeasure, enjoyed discussing with her brother Austin the possibility of reincarnation. By thirty she had stopped going to church, stating to her cousins Louise and Frances Norcross, "Let Emily sing for you because she cannot pray." Referring to herself as a "pagan," she wrote, "Who has not found the Heaven – below – /Will fail of it above." Two years before her death she admitted that " 'Consider the lilies' " was "the only Commandment I ever obeyed."

It is important to remember that in her strongest hours, Dickinson truly became a light unto herself. She once proclaimed:

> On a Columnar Self —
> How ample to rely
> In Tumult — or Extremity —
> How good the Certainty
> That Lever cannot pry —
> And Wedge cannot divide
> Conviction — That Granitic Base —
> Though None be on our Side — . . .

In her more fragile hours, however, she was obsessed with the inevitability of loss and death, haunted by the idea of eternity, tempted by the promise of immortality. Recalling a conversation he had with her in 1871, Dickinson's sometime mentor T. W. Higginson remarked: "When I said I would come again *some time* she said, 'Say in a long time, that will be nearer. Some time is nothing.'" To John L. Groves she reflected on *"wings* half gone to dust, that fluttered so, last year — a mouldering plume, an empty house, in which a bird resided. Where last year's flies, their errand ran, and last year's *crickets fell!* We, too, are flying — fading, John — and the song 'here lies,' soon upon lips that love us now — will have hummed and ended." To Mrs. Samuel Bowles she appealed: "This world is just a little place, just the red in the sky, before the sun rises, so let us keep fast hold of hands, that when the birds begin, none of us be missing." Like a child in a fairy tale, she was afraid of abandonment, separation, and the dark:

> *Adrift! A little boat adrift!*
> *And night is coming down!*

Yet there is another Emily Dickinson who declared: "The shore is safer, but I love to buffet the sea." It is this Emily who, already at the age of sixteen, was able occasionally to relax her anxious grip on passing time, writing to her friend Abiah Root: "Let us strive together to part with time more reluctantly, to watch the pinions of the fleeting moment until they are dim in the distance & the new coming moment claims our attention. . . . Earth is short[,] Abiah, but Paradise is *long,* there must be many moments in an eternal day — then *sometime we* shall tarry, while time and tide *roll on . . ."* About fifteen years later, having decided to stop attending church, Dickinson announced:

> *. . . Some keep the Sabbath in Surplice —*
> *I just wear my Wings —*

And instead of tolling the Bell, for Church,
Our little Sexton — sings.

God preaches, a noted Clergyman —
And the sermon is never long,
So instead of Getting to Heaven, at last —
I'm going, all along.

All the way to heaven was heaven; and the poet found her heaven on earth just outside her kitchen door—"The Prairie before the Door," she called it. Here, in her garden and orchard whose teeming life she studied and meditated on, Emily Dickinson found "exstasy in living" and learned to "eat evanescence slowly." It was her harborage, her spiritual retreat, the one place where she was at home in the universe. As she wrote in two famous letters to T. W. Higginson:

> You ask of my Companions Hills – Sir – and the Sundown – and a Dog large as myself, that my Father bought me – They are better than Beings because they know – but do not tell. . . .
> Of "shunning Men and Women" – they talk of Hallowed things, aloud – and embarrass my Dog – He and I dont object to them, if

they'll exist their side. I think Carlo [Emily's dog] would please you — He is dumb, and brave — I think you would like the Chestnut Tree I met in my walk. It hit my notice suddenly — and I thought the Skies were in Blossom —

Then there's a noiseless noise in the Orchard — that I let persons hear — ...

And in Dickinson's letters we often come across statements like the following: "Life is the finest secret. So long as that remains, we must all whisper.... All we secure of beauty is its evanescences.... No dreaming can compare with reality, for reality itself is a dream from which but a portion of mankind have yet waked and part of us is not a familiar peninsula."

Sentiments like the above could similarly have come from the pen of the seventeenth-century Matsuo Bashō, the greatest of the Japanese haiku poets, who became a recluse at fifty, living on the outskirts of Edo in a hut he called "Unreal Dwelling." Bashō wrote: "Indeed it is true that all the delusions of the senses are summed up in the one word *unreality*, and there is no way to forget even for a moment change and its swiftness.... My solitude shall be my company, and my poverty my wealth." One of his famous haiku reads:

Come, see
real flowers
of this painful world

It suggests a sense of life that Bashō shared with any number of Zen
Buddhist poets.

Zen, a school of Mahāyana Buddhism, was introduced into China
from India in the sixth and seventh centuries A.D. Its name, which
derives from the Chinese word *ch'an* and the Sanskrit word *dhyāna,*
refers in its largest sense to what has been called "the primordial
perfection of everything existing" and "the perfection present in
every person at every moment." Zen is considered a special
transmission outside the orthodox Buddhist teaching; it has been called
"a Buddha-teaching from heart-mind to heart-mind," much like what
took place when Shākyamuni Buddha held up a flower and his
disciple Kāshyapa smiled. (It is said that Kāshyapa himself became
the first patriarch of Zen in a lineage of transmission that, with the
influence of Taoist philosophy, eventually led to Ch'an Buddhism in
China and to the Rinzai and Soto schools of Zen still active today
in Japan.) In practice, Zen emphasizes the primary importance of *zazen*
(sitting meditation) as the most direct way to the experience of
enlightenment and minimizes the usefulness of ritual religious

practices, intellectual analysis, and sacred scriptures in attaining such enlightenment.

For her part, Emily Dickinson could not embrace the traditional Christian idea of faith, which, as the Bible says, "gives substance to our hopes, and makes us certain of realities we do not see." As she wrote:

> *The going from a world we know*
> *To one a wonder still*
> *Is like the child's adversity*
> *Whose vista is a hill,*
> *Behind the hill is sorcery*
> *And everything unknown,*
> *But will the secret compensate*
> *For climbing it alone?*

Rather she came to adopt an attitude of watchfulness and attention that allowed her, in Zen terms, to "awaken to the instant," to become aware of the *moment* that partakes of the absolute. "Infinite," said a Zen master, "is in the finite of each instant." "Forever," said Dickinson, "is composed of Nows."

One morning in her orchard the poet observed the dew in the grass. She wrote:

> *Dew — is the Freshet in the Grass —*
> *'Tis many a tiny Mill*
> *Turns unperceived beneath our feet*
> *And Artisan lies still*
>
> *We spy the Forests and the Hills*
> *The Tents to Nature's Show*
> *Mistake the Outside for the in*
> *And mention what we saw.*
>
> *Could Commentators on the Sign*
> *Of Nature's Caravan*
> *Obtain "Admission" as a Child*
> *Some Wednesday Afternoon.*

In *Zen Mind, Beginner's Mind* the late Zen Master Shunryu Suzuki states: "If your mind is empty, it is always ready for anything; it is open to everything. In the beginner's mind there are many possibilities; in the expert's mind there are few." It was with the childlike, beginner's mind that Emily obtained "admission" to the life in her orchard ("How happy is the little Stone/That rambles in the Road alone"; "For Captain was the Butterfly/For Helmsman was the Bee"; "A fuzzy fellow, without feet,/Yet doth exceding run!"). The orchard was her *temenos,* her sacred grove, where her soul and imagination were "at play." Here she tested and experimented with the sounds, smells, and tastes of words and, like a child, word-painted with the colors of Nature as if she were discovering them for the first time:

> *A slash of Blue —*
> *A sweep of Gray —*
> *Some scarlet patches on the way,*
> *Compose an evening Sky —*
> *A little purple — slipped between —*
> *Some Ruby Trousers hurried on —*
> *A Wave of Gold —*
> *A Bank of Day —*
> *This just makes out the Morning Sky.*

It was also in her orchard that she learned how to look not just *at* things but *as* them—an essential practice of Zen. Those familiar with Dickinson's poetry know that she often *used* nature—in the form of homilies ("Partake as doth the Bee,/Abstemiously"), definitions ("Presentiment – is that long Shadow – on the Lawn –/Indicative that Suns go down –"), and allegories (" 'Hope' is the thing with feathers –/That perches in the soul –"). Sometimes, too, she tried to *define* Nature (" 'Nature' is what we see –/The Hill – the Afternoon –/ . . . Nature is what we hear –/The Bobolink – the Sea –/ . . . Nature is what we know –/Yet have no art to say . . ."). Here the poet "says" what she says cannot be told . . . yet she is, of course, one of Nature's greatest hearers and seers. In her clearest moments she became what Ralph Waldo Emerson called "a transparent eyeball," allowed everything to become her teacher, and unknowingly followed the advice that Matsuo Bashō gave to the poets of his age:

> Go to the pine if you want to learn about the pine, or to the bamboo if you want to learn about the bamboo. And in doing so, you must leave your subjective preoccupation with yourself. Otherwise you impose yourself on the object and do not learn. Your poetry issues of its own accord when you and the object have become one—when you have plunged deep enough into the object to see something like a hidden glimmering there. However well phrased your poetry may be, if your feeling is not natural—if the object and yourself are separate—

then your poetry is not true poetry but merely your subjective counterfeit.

The Zen aesthetic valued the qualities of simplicity, naturalness, concision, imperfection, humor, stillness, and freedom; and each poem had its dominant mood: *sabi* (isolation), *wabi* (poverty), *aware* (impermanence), or *yugen* (mystery). Emily Dickinson did not write tanka or haiku (although her poem "Soft as the massacre of Suns/ By Evening's Sabre's slain" has the effect of the latter). Like the Japanese Zen poets she wrote about autumn moons, sunsets, snowstorms, fireflies, and dew but not about chrysanthemums, lotuses, plum blossoms, and bamboo (not popular staples of the Connecticut River Valley). Yet in her own inimitable, idiosyncratic manner she often expressed the aesthetic and mood of Zen poetry, which, incidentally, valued individual style. In the words of a Japanese Zen folk saying: "The One Mind/Of heaven and earth/Is dyed into/ A thousand different/Grass colors."

When challenged by T. W. Higginson about the unorthodox nature of her poetry, Dickinson replied: "All men say 'What' to me . . . [and] I have no Tribunal." Simply, she had to rely on her Columnar Self. Shunryu Suzuki states: "There is no certain way that exists permanently. There is no way set up for us. Moment after moment we have to find our own way. Some idea of perfection, or some perfect way which is set up by someone else, is not the true way for us. Each one of us must make his own true way, and when we do, that way will express the universal way."

Emily Dickinson's appropriation of the traditional meters of Congregational hymns—much as the composer Charles Ives used New England hymn tunes in his revolutionary compositions—provided the ground bass of her characteristic song. Sometimes calm, sometimes candent, it is a music that features a remarkable juxtaposition of elements: a jumpy, breathless prosody that she referred to as her "spasmodic gait" and described as the "bells whose jingling cooled my tramp"; a use of continually surprising slant, near, and accidental rhymes; and both a Shakespearean richness of language and a nursery-rhyme simplicity and humor. Along with its ideographic presentation of images and ideas, Dickinson's verse reveals a microscopic enlargement of the processes of nature, as if from the perspective of a grasshopper or butterfly, as well as a charmed, curious openness to the erotic encounters between bees and flowers, meadows and sun. Most striking is her unique punctuation, whose profuseness of dashes suggests, among other things, the hesitating and quickening stresses of the poet's breathing, the attempt to arrest time, and the conduction of new circuits of thought. Finally, the Dickinsonian music expresses what the American poet William Carlos Williams called "a swiftness impaling beauty . . . a rapidity too swift for touch."

In her verse Emily Dickinson was able to catch the "suchness" and "nowness" of robins, bats, mushrooms, spiders, stones, snakes, dandelions, hummingbirds, dawns, and summer showers. From them she experienced "Glory," "Awe," "Ecstasy," "Glee," "Rapture," "Joy," "Bliss," and from them she learned how to exist in her true mind. ("Your true mind," said Shunryu Suzuki, "is always with whatever you see.") There was no need for Dickinson to journey anywhere. She declared: "To shut our eyes is Travel. The Seasons understand this." Standing in solitude and silence she sensed that any moment might open the door to infinity and reveal heaven in a wildflower.

It is told that the Greek goddess Persephone was one day gathering flowers in a meadow when, stretching out her hand to pluck a bright narcissus, she was snatched by Hades, lord of the underworld, and taken by him to live in the realm of the dead. Like the goddess, Emily Dickinson also fell from ecstasy into despair, over and over again. At sixteen she wrote a friend: "When I am most happy, there is a sting in every enjoyment. I find no rose without a thorn." In a poem she declared: "For each ecstatic intant/We must an anguish pay." As the depth psychologist James Hillman writes: "The Persephone experience occurs to us each in sudden depressions . . . drawn downward out of life by a force we cannot see, against which we would flee, distractedly thrashing about for naturalistic explanations and comforts for what is happening so darkly. We feel invaded from below, assaulted, and we think of death."

Today, Emily Dickinson would probably be diagnosed as a borderline personality or as suffering from a bipolar disorder. Certainly she knew her mind was often a haunted place ("Ourself behind ourself, concealed —/Should startle me —"). But as the Tibetan Buddhist doctor Lobsang Rapgay has stated: "For the Buddhist, the mind is a state of awareness, the ability to perceive or be aware of whatever it is experiencing—itself, as well as objects external to itself. . . . The mind then becomes an unbiased, unprejudiced reflecting agent, totally nonjudgmental, and you begin to approach your life and illness with that attitude. For example, you see anxiety as just another experience in the vast expanse of the psyche, merely being hosted by consciousness—appearing, lasting for a duration, then dissolving back into its own base, the mind."

Even after her breakdowns, Emily Dickinson was able to write about them with astonishing clarity and dispassion, observing the motions of her "glittering Retinue of nerves," as she called them, much the way she watched spiders unwinding their "Yarns of Pearl":

I felt a Cleaving in my Mind —
As if my Brain had split —
I tried to match it — Seam by Seam —
But could not make them fit.

The thought behind, I strove to join
Unto the thought before —
But Sequence ravelled out of Sound
Like Balls — upon a Floor.

For Dickinson, the writing of such a poem—and there were many others like it—was a kind of anodyne for her experience of dissociation and dissolution, enabling her to recollect herself. Indeed, one might see Dickinson's sewing of her individual poems together into little fascicle-booklets—for this is the way she preserved them—as a kind of suturing of her psychic wounds. The "balsam word" of poetry, as she termed it, was her salvation, a practice of mindfulness that served to heal a broken consciousness and to remind her that, as she once declared, *"My* business is to love. . . . *My* business is to *sing — ,"*

In *Skies in Blossom* I have chosen to present a group of Emily Dickinson's poems in which, with a beginner's mind, she regards the natural world in ways that honor the "beingness" of nature. The poems are, in any case, luminous, timeless works that require no special justification for being published together. One could, however, also put together a similarly sized collection of Dickinson's poems focusing on what she referred to as her "nervous prostrations," in which she unflinchingly examines the nature of her mind. Such a volume, too, would reveal Dickinson as a Zen poet because she did not observe perspicaciously and write accurately only about the bursting of a chrysalis or the sun rising "a Ribbon at a time." In both outer and inner nature, she discovered and paid attention to her many selves ("Blossoms of the Brain")—of pain and bliss, darkness and light, fear and surrender. And there were many Emilys, each of them in awe of the ineffable wonder and mystery of existence, each of them silently holding up a flower. In the words of the thirteenth-century Master Dōgen: "To learn the way of the Buddha is to learn about oneself. To learn about oneself is to forget oneself. To forget oneself is to be enlightened by everything in the world. To be enlightened by everything is to let fall one's own body and mind."

NOTE: The forty-three poems in *Skies in Blossom* are reproduced here in the chronological order that they appear in *The Complete Poems of Emily Dickinson,* edited by Thomas H. Johnson. In her life's "journey toward Circumference," Emily Dickinson observed and experienced things in panoptic fashion and often wrote many poems apiece, for example, on various flowers, birds, insects, as well as on subjects such as dawns and sunsets (no two of which are ever the same). I have therefore included poems on similar subjects when they revealed different facets and aspects of the subject, different ways of Emily Dickinson's seeing and saying "The simple News that Nature told."

South Winds jostle them —
Bumblebees come —
Hover — hesitate —
Drink, and are gone —

Butterflies pause
On their passage Cashmere —
I — softly plucking,
Present them here!

A fuzzy fellow, without feet,
Yet doth exceeding run!
Of velvet, is his Countenance,
And his Complexion, dun!

Sometime, he dwelleth in the grass!
Sometime, upon a bough,
From which he doth descend in plush
Upon the Passer-by!

All this in summer.
But when winds alarm the Forest Folk,
He taketh *Damask* Residence —
And struts in sewing silk!

Then, finer than a Lady,
Emerges in the spring!
A Feather on each shoulder!
You'd scarce recognize him!

By Men, yclept Caterpillar!
By me! But who am I,
To tell the pretty secret
Of the Butterfly!

A slash of Blue —
A sweep of Gray —
Some scarlet patches on the way,
Compose an Evening Sky —
A little purple — slipped between —
Some Ruby Trousers hurried on —
A Wave of Gold —
A Bank of Day —
This just makes out the Morning Sky.

Blazing in Gold and quenching in Purple
Leaping like Leopards to the Sky
Then at the feet of the old Horizon
Laying her spotted Face to die
Stooping as low as the Otter's Window
Touching the Roof and tinting the Barn
Kissing her Bonnet to the Meadow
And the Juggler of Day is gone

Where Ships of Purple – gently toss –
On Seas of Daffodil –
Fantastic Sailors – mingle –
And then – the Wharf is still!

I'll tell you how the Sun rose —
A Ribbon at a time —
The Steeples swam in Amethyst —
The news, like Squirrels, ran —
The Hills untied their Bonnets —
The Bobolinks — begun —
Then I said softly to myself —
"That must have been the Sun"!
But how he set — I know not —
There seemed a purple stile
That little Yellow boys and girls
Were climbing all the while —
Till when they reached the other side,
A Dominie in Gray —
Put gently up the evening Bars —
And led the flock away —

A Bird came down the Walk —
He did not know I saw —
He bit an Angleworm in halves
And ate the fellow, raw,

And then he drank a Dew
From a convenient Grass —
And then hopped sidewise to the Wall
To let a Beetle pass —

He glanced with rapid eyes
That hurried all around —
They looked like frightened Beads, I thought —
He stirred his Velvet Head

Like one in danger, Cautious,
I offered him a Crumb
And he unrolled his feathers
And rowed him softer home —

Than Oars divide the Ocean,
Too silver for a seam —
Or Butterflies, off Banks of Noon
Leap, plashless as they swim.

The Grass so little has to do –
A Sphere of simple Green –
With only Butterflies to brood
And Bees to entertain –

And stir all day to pretty Tunes
The Breezes fetch along –
And hold the Sunshine in its lap
And bow to everything –

And thread the Dews, all night, like Pearls –
And make itself so fine
A Duchess were too common
For such a noticing –

And even when it dies – to pass
In Odors so divine –
Like Lowly spices, lain to sleep –
Or Spikenards, perishing –

And then, in Sovereign Barns to dwell –
And dream the Days away,
The Grass so little has to do
I wish I were a Hay –

Through the Dark Sod – as Education –
The Lily passes sure –
Feels her white foot – no trepidation –
Her faith – no fear –

Afterward – in the Meadow –
Swinging her Beryl Bell –
The Mold-life – all forgotten – now –
In Ecstasy – and Dell –

Within my Garden, rides a Bird
Upon a single Wheel —
Whose spokes a dizzy Music make
As 'twere a travelling Mill —

He never stops, but slackens
Above the Ripest Rose —
Partakes without alighting
And praises as he goes,

Till every spice is tasted —
And then his Fairy Gig
Reels in remoter atmospheres —
And I rejoin my Dog,

And He and I, perplex us
If positive, 'twere we —
Or bore the Garden in the Brain
This Curiosity —

But He, the best Logician,
Refers my clumsy eye —
To just vibrating Blossoms!
An Exquisite Reply!

The Black Berry — wears a Thorn in his side —
But no Man heard Him cry —
He offers His Berry, just the same
To Partridge — and to Boy —

He sometimes holds upon the Fence —
Or struggles to a Tree —
Or clasps a Rock, with both His Hands —
But not for Sympathy —

We — tell a Hurt — to cool it —
This Mourner — to the Sky
A little further reaches — instead —
Brave Black Berry —

The Spider holds a Silver Ball
In unperceived Hands —
And dancing softly to Himself
His Yarn of Pearl — unwinds —

He plies from Nought to Nought —
In unsubstantial Trade —
Supplants our Tapestries with His —
In half the period —

An Hour to rear supreme
His Continents of Light —
Then dangle from the Housewife's Broom —
His Boundaries — forgot —

629

I watched the Moon around the House
Until upon a Pane —
She stopped — a Traveller's privilege — for Rest —
And there upon

I gazed — as at a stranger —
The Lady in the Town
Doth think no incivility
To lift her Glass — upon —

But never Stranger justified
The Curiosity
Like Mine — for not a Foot — nor Hand —
Nor Formula — had she —

But like a Head — a Guillotine
Slid carelessly away —
Did independent, Amber —
Sustain her in the sky —

Or like a Stemless Flower —
Upheld in rolling Air

By finer Gravitations —
Than bind Philosopher —

No Hunger — had she — nor an Inn —
Her Toilette — to suffice —
Nor Avocation — nor Concern
For little Mysteries

As harass us — like Life — and Death —
And Afterwards — or Nay —
But seemed engrossed to Absolute —
With shining — and the Sky —

The privilege to scrutinize
Was scarce upon my Eyes
When, with a Silver practise —
She vaulted out of Gaze —

And next — I met her on a Cloud —
Myself too far below
To follow her superior Road —
Or its advantage — Blue —

The name – of it – is "Autumn" –
The hue – of it – is Blood –
An Artery – upon the Hill –
A Vein – along the Road –

Great Globules – in the Alleys –
And Oh, the Shower of Stain –
When Winds – upset the Basin –
And spill the Scarlet Rain –

It sprinkles Bonnets – far below –
It gathers ruddy Pools –
Then – eddies like a Rose – away –
Upon Vermilion Wheels –

The Moon was but a Chin of Gold
A Night or two ago –
And now she turns Her perfect Face
Upon the World below –

Her Forehead is of Amplest Blonde –
Her Cheek – a Beryl hewn –
Her Eye unto the Summer Dew
The likest I have known –

Her Lips of Amber never part –
But what must be the smile
Upon Her Friend she could confer
Were such Her Silver Will –

And what a privilege to be
But the remotest Star –
For Certainty She take Her Way
Beside Your Palace Door –

Her Bonnet is the Firmament –
The Universe – Her Shoe –
The Stars – the Trinkets at Her Belt –
Her Dimities – of Blue –

The Mountains — grow unnoticed —
Their Purple figures rise
Without attempt — Exhaustion —
Assistance — or Applause —

In Their Eternal Faces
The Sun — with just delight
Looks long — and last — and golden —
For fellowship — at night —

A Drop fell on the Apple Tree —
Another — on the Roof —
A Half a Dozen kissed the Eaves —
And made the Gables laugh —

A few went out to help the Brook
That went to help the Sea —
Myself Conjectured were they Pearls —
What Necklaces could be —

The Dust replaced, in Hoisted Roads —
The Birds jocoser sung —
The Sunshine threw his Hat away —
The Bushes — spangles flung —

The Breezes brought dejected Lutes —
And bathed them in the Glee —
Then Orient showed a single Flag,
And signed the Fete away —

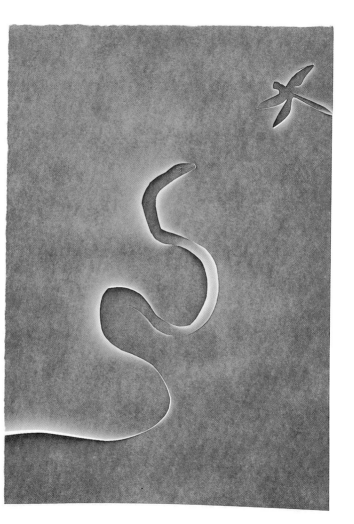

986

A narrow Fellow in the Grass
Occasionally rides –
You may have met Him – did you not
His notice sudden is –

The Grass divides as with a Comb –
A spotted shaft is seen –
And then it closes at your feet
And opens further on –

He likes a Boggy Acre
A Floor too cool for Corn –
Yet when a Boy, and Barefoot –
I more than once at Noon
Have passed, I thought, a Whip lash
Unbraiding in the Sun
When stooping to secure it
It wrinkled, and was gone –

Several of Nature's People
I know, and they know me –
I feel for them a transport
Of cordiality –

But never met this Fellow
Attended, or alone
Without a tighter breathing
And Zero at the Bone –

Bee! I'm expecting you!
Was saying Yesterday
To Somebody you know
That you were due —

The Frogs got Home last Week —
Are settled, and at work —
Birds, mostly back —
The Clover warm and thick —

You'll get my Letter by
The seventeenth; Reply
Or better, be with me —
Yours, Fly.

Like Men and Women Shadows walk
Upon the Hills Today —
With here and there a mighty Bow
Or trailing Courtesy
To Neighbors doubtless of their own
Not quickened to perceive
Minuter landscape as Ourselves
And Boroughs where we live —

1127

Soft as the massacre of Suns
By Evening's Sabres slain

A Spider sewed at Night
Without a Light
Upon an Arc of White.

If Ruff it was of Dame
Or Shroud of Gnome
Himself himself inform.

Of Immortality
His Strategy
Was Physiognomy.

The Day grew small, surrounded tight
By early, stooping Night —
The Afternoon in Evening deep
Its Yellow shortness dropt —
The Winds went out their martial ways
The Leaves obtained excuse —
November hung his Granite Hat
Upon a nail of Plush —

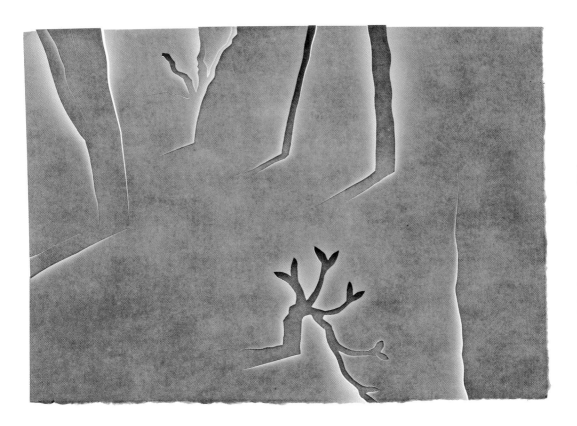

1198

A soft Sea washed around the House
A Sea of Summer Air
And rose and fell the magic Planks
That sailed without a care —
For Captain was the Butterfly
For Helmsman was the Bee
And an entire universe
For the delighted crew.

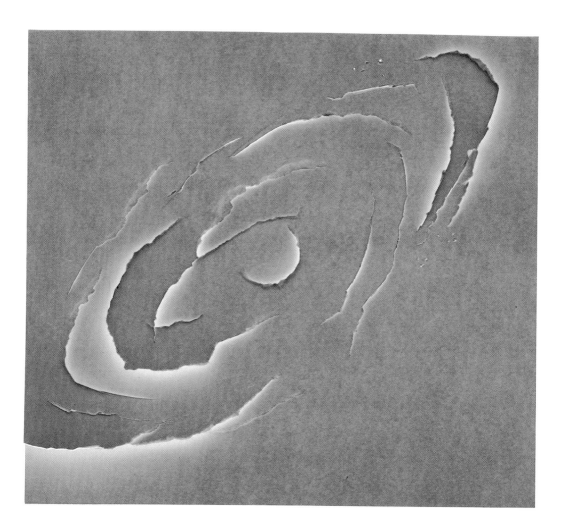

Like Rain it sounded till it curved
And then I knew 'twas Wind —
It walked as wet as any Wave
But swept as dry as sand —
When it had pushed itself away
To some remotest Plain
A coming as of Hosts was heard
That was indeed the Rain —
It filled the Wells, it pleased the Pools
It warbled in the Road —
It pulled the spigot from the Hills
And let the Floods abroad —
It loosened acres, lifted seas
The sites of Centres stirred
Then like Elijah rode away
Upon a Wheel of Cloud.

1265

The most triumphant Bird I ever knew or met
Embarked upon a twig today
And till Dominion set
I famish to behold so eminent a sight
And sang for nothing scrutable
But intimate Delight.
Retired, and resumed his transitive Estate —
To what delicious Accident
Does finest Glory fit!

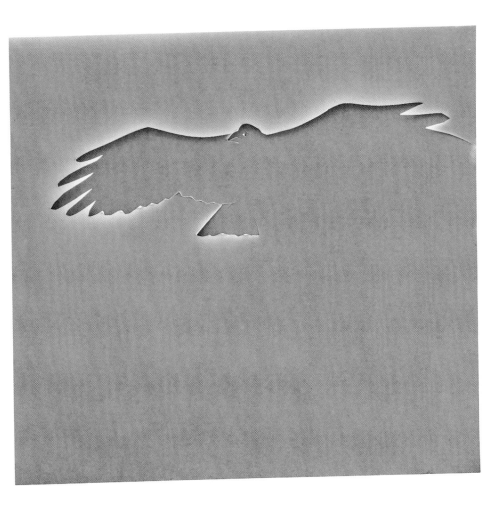

The Mushroom is the Elf of Plants —
At Evening, it is not —
At Morning, in a Truffled Hut
It stop upon a Spot

As if it tarried always
And yet its whole Career
Is shorter than a Snake's Delay
And fleeter than a Tare —

'Tis Vegetation's Juggler —
The Germ of Alibi —
Doth like a Bubble antedate
And like a Bubble, hie —

I feel as if the Grass was pleased
To have it intermit —
This surreptitious scion
Of Summer's circumspect.

Had Nature any supple Face
Or could she one contemn —
Had Nature an Apostate —
That Mushroom — it is Him!

Pink — small — and punctual —
Aromatic — low —
Covert — in April —
Candid — in May —
Dear to the Moss —
Known to the Knoll —
Next to the Robin
In every human Soul —
Bold little Beauty
Bedecked with thee
Nature forswears
Antiquity —

A Bee his burnished Carriage
Drove boldly to a Rose —
Combinedly alighting —
Himself — his Carriage was —
The Rose received his visit
With frank tranquillity
Withholding not a Crescent
To his Cupidity —
Their Moment consummated —
Remained for him — to flee —
Remained for her — of rapture
But the humility.

Bees are Black, with Gilt Surcingles —
Buccaneers of Buzz.
Ride abroad in ostentation
And subsist on Fuzz.

Fuzz ordained — not Fuzz contingent —
Marrows of the Hill.
Jugs — a Universe's fracture
Could not jar or spill.

1448

How soft a Caterpillar steps —
I find one on my Hand
From such a velvet world it comes
Such plushes at command
Its soundless travels just arrest
My slow — terrestrial eye
Intent upon its own career
What use has it for me —

1463

A Route of Evanescence
With a revolving Wheel –
A Resonance of Emerald –
A Rush of Cochineal –
And every Blossom on the Bush
Adjusts its tumbled Head –
The mail from Tunis, probably,
An easy Morning's Ride –

Before you thought of Spring
Except as a Surmise
You see — God bless his suddenness —
A Fellow in the Skies
Of independent Hues
A little weather worn
Inspiriting habiliments
Of Indigo and Brown —
With specimens of Song
As if for you to choose —
Discretion in the interval
With gay delays he goes
To some superior Tree
Without a single Leaf
And shouts for joy to Nobody
But his seraphic self —

1510

How happy is the little Stone
That rambles in the Road alone,
And doesn't care about Careers
And Exigencies never fears —
Whose Coat of elemental Brown
A passing Universe put on,
And independent as the Sun
Associates or glows alone,
Fulfilling absolute Decree
In casual simplicity —

1513

"Go traveling with us!"
Her travels daily be
By routes of ecstasy
To Evening's Sea —

1519

The Dandelion's pallid tube
Astonishes the Grass,
And Winter instantly becomes
An infinite Alas —

The tube uplifts a signal Bud
And then a shouting Flower, —
The Proclamation of the Suns
That sepulture is o'er.

1520

The stem of a departed Flower
Has still a silent rank.
The Bearer from an Emerald Court
Of a Despatch of Pink.

1526

His oriental heresies
Exhilarate the Bee,
And filling all the Earth and Air
With gay apostasy
Fatigued at last, a Clover plain
Allures his jaded eye
That lowly Breast where Butterflies
Have felt it meet to die —

1540

As imperceptibly as Grief
The Summer lapsed away —
Too imperceptible at last
To seem like Perfidy —
A Quietness distilled
As Twilight long begun,
Or Nature spending with herself
Sequestered Afternoon —
The Dusk drew earlier in —
The Morning foreign shone —
A courteous, yet harrowing Grace,
As Guest, that would be gone —
And thus, without a Wing
Or service of a Keel
Our Summer made her light escape
Into the Beautiful.

No Brigadier throughout the Year
So civic as the Jay —
A Neighbor and a Warrior too
With shrill felicity
Pursuing Winds that censure us
A February Day,
The Brother of the Universe
Was never blown away —
The Snow and he are intimate —
I've often seen them play
When Heaven looked upon us all
With such severity
I felt apology were due
To an insulted sky
Whose pompous frown was Nutriment
To their Temerity —
The Pillow of this daring Head
Is pungent Evergreens —
His Larder — terse and Militant —
Unknown — refreshing things —
His Character — a Tonic —
His Future — a Dispute —
Unfair an Immortality
That leaves this Neighbor out —

The Bat is dun, with wrinkled Wings —
Like fallow Article —
And not a song pervade his Lips —
Or none perceptible.

His small Umbrella quaintly halved
Describing in the Air
An Arc alike inscrutable
Elate Philosopher.

Deputed from what Firmament —
Of what Astute Abode —
Empowered with what Malignity
Auspiciously withheld —

To his adroit Creator
Ascribe no less the praise —
Beneficent, believe me,
His Eccentricities —

There came a Wind like a Bugle —
It quivered through the Grass
And a Green Chill upon the Heat
So ominous did pass
We barred the Windows and the Doors
As from an Emerald Ghost —
The Doom's electric Moccasin
That very instant passed —
On a strange Mob of panting Trees
And Fences fled away
And Rivers where the Houses ran
Those looked that lived — that Day —
The Bell within the steeple wild
The flying tidings told —
How much can come
And much can go,
And yet abide the World!

1606

Quite empty, quite at rest,
The Robin locks her Nest, and tries her Wings.
She does not know a Route
But puts her Craft about
For *rumored* Springs –
She does not ask for Noon –
She does not ask for Boon,
Crumbless and homeless, of but one request –
The Birds she lost –

call these images shadow papers because they exist on account of light, and there's no shadow without light. They're pieces of paper that are cut with a scissor. I hold them up to the light and cut freely— it's a kind of dance with the paper. I try to find forms and create space without cutting anything out of the paper.

I wanted each image to be as austere and yet full as Emily Dickinson's poems. She can take the most wrenching feelings and put them into five or six words. What an ability—to bring the outside world in and the inside world out to meet it! They meet in these words that are helpless looking and yet so strong.

My shadow papers come alive only when they are held up to light. Then, gravity pulls on the masses I have cut free from the sheet, and the papers gradually open, letting in the light that gives them form. The pieces of cut paper range in size from $5 \frac{1}{2}$ inches by 6 inches to 12 inches by 17 inches. The photographer Jerry Thompson has collaborated with me, discussing and photographing my work for this book. In his photographs my shadow papers blossom into full life.

—MARY FRANK

Thanks to Scott Moyers and Marysarah Quinn for their help in editing and designing *Skies in Blossom.* Special thanks to Mrs. Maj Nilsson for allowing me to use her little Zen cottage in Kattvik (Skåne), Sweden, where I was able to think and write about Emily Dickinson in the summer of 1994.

—JONATHAN COTT